Together, our love for staying positive, our shared life experiences, and our unwavering belief that words and mindset are power. We wrote this book to help you become the best version of yourself.

Thank you to everyone who's been a part of our journey.

From Texroy:

To my Mom, Eunice Turner, my rock, and my Dad, Joseph Elliott, who's always been there for me. Big shout-out to my siblings: Althea, Wayne, Lerone, and Lacresia Elliott. You guys have always got my back.

To my kids, who mean the world to me: Xye Elliott, Alexxus Elliott, Texroy Elliott Jr, my grandkids Nova, Kroy, and Navy Rayno.

From Erika:

To my kids, my joys, Olivia and Gigi Vassell. In honor of my Mom, Abuela Lynne, who is now our Angel. Her positive vibes have shaped so much in this book.

And my Grandpa Charles who taught me the Seven T's in life. Take the Time to Think Things Through.

INTRODUCTION

In a world that constantly demands our time and attention, how often do we give ourselves the chance to pause, reflect, and recharge? Every day presents a new challenge. A new hurdle to overcome. A new opportunity to be seized. Wouldn't it be powerful if we had a tool to provide us with a daily dose of inspiration and energy to meet those challenges head-on?

Welcome to ***Your Daily Boost 365***.

Texroy Elliott and Erika Bowes-Vassell, two formidable minds with a shared history, have come together to offer you just that. Through their combined experiences, wisdom, and deep-rooted conviction that every individual possesses an untapped reservoir of potential, they bring to you 365 insights—each day, a new beacon of inspiration.

Growing up and throughout their lives

Texroy and Erika experienced firsthand the importance of resilience, motivation, and the indomitable human spirit. They've witnessed the power of mindset in turning challenges into stepping stones, and with this book, they invite you to experience the same transformation.

The essence of Your Daily Boost 365 isn't just about feeling good momentarily. It's about embedding positive, proactive

INTRODUCTION

behaviors and beliefs into your life. It's about recognizing that motivation isn't merely a fleeting emotion but a habit that can be cultivated and harnessed.

Each page you turn will introduce you to a mantra or insight carefully crafted to empower, uplift, and propel you forward. Some days, the words might challenge you, nudging you out of your comfort zone, while others might offer solace and understanding. But every single day, they will aim to ignite a fire within.

This book is not just another collection of quotes. It's a daily mentor, a silent partner, and a steadfast friend. It's your compass on days you feel lost and your anchor on days you feel overwhelmed.

In *Your Daily Boost 365*, you are not alone. With Texroy and Erika as your guides, be prepared to embrace each day with renewed vigor, passion, and determination. Open this book with an open heart, and witness the unfolding of a more confident, empowered, and successful version of yourself.

Now, let the journey begin!

Texroy and Erika

It makes no sense to worry about death because you don't know when it's your time, so live your life to the fullest and enjoy.

Priorities come 1st.

Work hard, play later.

Pay attention to what makes your heart smile.

YOUR DAILY BOOST

Does this truly impact my life, or am I caught up in emotions?

Remember where you were before you took action and changed.

Celebrate the small action steps because they make a big impact when they are repeated.

Stress will take your beauty away.

Words are power.

⚡

Are you worried about the wrong things?

Always stay focused. That's a fact, or you will not be successful.

Happiness in life is having someone strong in the areas you are weak.

YOUR DAILY BOOST

Time is the master of everything.

It is what it is.

Always remain humble.

humble

Take advantage of the time you got.

People fear what they don't understand.

People hate what they can't conquer.

Common sense is the best sense that you have.

Not everyone knows how to use common sense.

Know your worth.

YOUR DAILY BOOST

Nobody pays attention to the warning label until it's too late (this applies to people).

It's your story. Tell it any way you want.

Could be till whenever or Could be forever.

If you are strong in life, you will always be good.

You won't be stressed when you love yourself enough to let nothing bother you.

You should know your worth, and I should know mine.

Pay close attention to your words as they become what you attract.

Always do the necessary things.

Always think positive even in a negative situation.

Are you wishing and dreaming or taking the daily necessary steps?

Stop overanalyzing and view the situation from the lens of. "It is what it is."

Dream

What did you do today to get closer to your dream life?

Are you reminding yourself daily of your past mistakes or telling yourself how amazing you are?

Proper Planning Prevents Poor Performance.

You have to be able to stay focused long enough to be successful.

Keep your morals and principles intact.

Believe in yourself when no one else does.

Don't let anyone interfere with your work.

Think big.

When you look in the mirror, focus on the positive qualities.

When a negative thought enters your head, pretend it's a balloon and pop that negativity immediately.

Make a point to be a blessing to others.

Embrace the journey of your life, not just the end goal.

Dare to dream bigger than ever before. It's exciting.

Your past doesn't define your future.

Take risks and live without regrets.

Find joy in the simplest activities.

Learn from your mistakes and grow stronger.

Step outside your comfort zone and discover you were meant to shine.

Embrace change and adapt with grace.

Believe in your own potential and abilities.

Choose happiness over perfection.

YOUR DAILY BOOST

Be the architect of your destiny.

Create a life that feels like a masterpiece.

Focus on progress, not perfection.

Find beauty in chaos.

Be grateful for what you have while working towards what you want.

Chase experiences, not possessions.

Embrace solitude and discover yourself.

Live in the present moment, for it is all we truly have.

Celebrate the small victories along the way.

Let go of what no longer serves you.

Believe in miracles and create your own.

Surround yourself with positive and uplifting people.

Explore the unknown with curiosity and wonder.

Dance to the rhythm of your own heart.

Practice self-compassion and kindness.

Pursue your passions and let them light your path.

Stand tall, even in the face of adversity.

Treat failure as a bump in the road. It's not the end-all.

Find inspiration in nature's beauty.

Nurture your mind, body, and soul.

Make peace with your past and embrace forgiveness.

Be the change you wish to see in the world.

Stay true to your values, even when it's difficult.

Not everyone deserves your time.

Live authentically and be true to yourself.

Practice gratitude daily to grow your positive mindset.

Believe that anything is possible with determination and hard work.

Find your purpose and live with passion.

Release the need for external validation.

Trust the timing of your life's journey.

Seek knowledge and never stop learning.

Embrace uncertainty as an opportunity for growth.

Choose love over fear in every situation.

Be a source of light and positivity in the world.

Embody resilience and bounce back from challenges.

Find inspiration in the success of others.

Dare to be different and embrace your uniqueness.

Let go of comparison and focus on your own progress.

Practice self-care and prioritize your well-being.

Follow your gut feeling, your inner voice.
Has it let you down before?

Cultivate meaningful relationships that lift you up.

Find the balance between work, play, and rest.

Celebrate your strengths and embrace your weaknesses.

Embrace the power of gratitude to transform your life.

Cultivate a positive mindset and watch your world change.

Practice forgiveness for yourself and others.

Let go of the need for control and enjoy the moment.

Keep moving forward, even when you need clarification on the destination.

Be open to new perspectives and ideas.

Speak your truth with love and kindness.

Believe in yourself, even when others doubt you.

Embrace challenges as opportunities for growth.

Take time to reflect and gain clarity on your priorities.

Seek adventure and explore the unknown.

Choose joy and laughter in every moment.

Foster a sense of curiosity and never stop asking questions.

Practice patience and trust the process.

Embrace imperfections and find beauty in them.

Celebrate your progress, no matter how small.

Live with integrity and honor your values.

Find inspiration in the beauty of everyday life.

Embrace the power of self-love and self-acceptance.

Find your voice and use it to make a difference.

Let go of expectations and embrace what is.

Believe in unlimited possibilities of the universe.

Face your fears head-on and watch them dissolve.

Seek out those who have come before you and learn from their wisdom.

Stay curious and never stop exploring.

Find peace in solitude and silence.

Take responsibility for your own happiness.

Trust that everything happens for a reason.

Be kind to yourself and others.

Find inspiration in the stories of resilience and triumph.

Practice self-reflection to gain deeper insights about yourself.

Let go of attachments and find freedom.

Take inspired action and watch your dreams come to life.

Embrace the power of gratitude to transform your perspective.

Stay true to your authentic self, no matter the circumstances.

Embrace the unknown and let it fuel your curiosity.

Let go of judgment and practice acceptance.

Invest in experiences that enrich your soul.

Seek simplicity and find beauty in the ordinary.

Trust your intuition, for it is your inner compass.

Find inspiration in the interconnectedness of all things.

Embrace the ebb and flow of life's cycles.

Let go of the need to be right and open your mind to new possibilities.

Practice mindfulness and bring awareness to the present moment.

Surround yourself with people who inspire and uplift you.

Find solace in nature and reconnect with its wisdom.

Choose love over hate, kindness over cruelty.

Live with intention and purpose in every action.

Plan time daily to be still and reflect on your accomplishments.

Allow yourself to be vulnerable and embrace your authenticity.

Find beauty in the process, not just the outcome.

Embrace the lessons that come from failure.

Leave your comfort zone and embrace that this will be new. It may be a bit painful, but so worth it.

YOUR DAILY BOOST

Believe in your own potential to create a meaningful life.

So what if you have a setback? You are still ahead of the game.

Shift your thoughts to look at the opportunities for learning and growth.

Choose compassion and empathy in your interactions.

Practice self-care to nourish your mind, body, and spirit.

Let go of regrets and focus on the present moment.

Surround yourself with positive influences.

Remember that every day is a fresh start.

Take responsibility for your own happiness and well-being.

Seek inspiration in the beauty of the natural world.

Embrace gratitude and cultivate a thankful heart.

Choose positivity and optimism in the face of challenges.

Celebrate your achievements, no matter how small.

Embrace the power of self-belief and confidence.

Find purpose in serving others.

Practice mindfulness to bring presence into your life.

Let go of what no longer serves your growth.

See failures as stepping stones to success.

Commitment to your goals is vital even when it gets tough.

Choose forgiveness and release the weight of the past.

Seek adventure and explore the world with curiosity.

Cultivate a supportive network of like-minded individuals.

Embrace the unknown and trust everything works out.

Choose joy as a way of life.

Find inspiration in the success stories of others.

Practice gratitude for the abundance in your life.

Take time for self-reflection and introspection.

Believe in the power of your dreams and aspirations.

Embrace and seek out opportunities for growth and learning.

Surround yourself with positive affirmations.

I believe in me

Find inspiration in the resilience of the human spirit.

Let go of limiting beliefs and embrace your true potential.

Choose love over fear in every decision you make.

Find inspiration in the beauty of diversity and inclusivity.

Practice self-discipline and consistency in pursuing your goals.

Celebrate your uniqueness and embrace your individuality.

Trust the process and have faith in your journey.

Find inspiration in the wisdom of those who came before you.

Gratitude

Embrace the power of gratitude to transform your mindset.

Keep an open mind and heart for the unknown while you approach with courage and curiosity.

YOUR DAILY BOOST

Let go of the need for approval and live on your terms.

Seek inspiration in the small miracles of everyday life.

Practice self-compassion and be gentle with yourself.

Believe in your ability to overcome any obstacle.

Celebrate life's blessings, big and small.

Do what makes sense.

Everything ain't for everybody.

Make a 3-year plan of skills you want to learn and check them off yearly. You will be surprised at what you have accomplished.

What's yours is yours.

When you sit around being miserable and unhappy, you are only hurting yourself.

Always try your best to be happy even when you are not supposed to be.

☺

The smart and strong ones live their life to the fullest and are happy.

Embrace the beauty of simplicity and minimalism.

Learn one step at a time. It's less overwhelming.

Celebrate your accomplishments even if you feel they are insignificant.

The small steps you take daily and repeat will build your business.

Pray and let go of negative things, people, and thoughts.

Every interaction with someone online or in person has the ability to be a blessing.

If you live in fear of dying, you are missing out on something beautiful.

Seek out the good in others.

A reminder to look at people's actions as they speak louder than words.

Live the life you love.

Love the life you live.

Set the trends. Don't follow them.

Love is the answer.

Look people in the eye vs. staring at your phone when chatting.

Love hard without strings attached.

Be open to meeting new people.

Rekindle relationships with a new lens.

Always treat people the way you would want to be treated-No double standards.

Be careful of assuming, as you never fully know what someone is dealing with.

Learn to love yourself first before entering a relationship.

Remember, your mood does not depend on who replies to your messages.

When you are ghosted, remember God removes people from your life.

Are you cheering for others?

What did you do in the past seven days to bring a smile to another human?

Seek the good in others but pay attention to the red flags.

Your tongue is powerful. Take a moment to pause before speaking.

When chatting, ask yourself if the shoe was on the other foot, how would I take this - Hmmmm?

Are you feeding your mind positive words even in the music you listen to?

Why do we feel being an Entrepreneur is a risk when working for someone else can end instantly?

TAKE the RISK

Life is about taking chances. That's how you get ahead.

Never let one person put your fire out.

You won't get as far if you focus on what's in it for yourself vs. what's in it for others.

Stay in your lane. This is your journey. God has a plan for you.

Keep your blinders on.

Stop It! Yes, Stop the negativity.

Plan your time; if you don't finish the task, add it to the next day. Keep adding it to the list until it's complete, even if it's a year.

Procrastination is a thief.

★★★★★

Plan to win or wing it and don't.

Find a partner who gets you.

Don't play dumb to fit in.

Don't try to fit in. That's crazy.
You were meant to shine.

Bless others daily.

Smile and shine bright.

Don't let that one "no" stop you, because a boatload of YESSES are on their way.

Don't allow a NO to stop you from serving others.

Your time is valuable and has a price.

Choose to seek the positive even in darkness.

Who cares what others say about you -haters will always be there. The key is not to allow them to derail you.

What do you want your legacy to be?

Even when the stars are not out, it's still your time to shine.

Even when the sun is out, you're still the shining star.

Take the trip, make memories, and enjoy the fruits of your labor.

Being curious shows, you care.

Asking questions is key.

Beware of making Assumptions.

Who are you allowing in your space?

You are here for a reason.

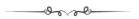

You have the solution. Pay attention.

Remember your childhood dreams?
Are there any you would like to revisit and achieve?

Do you want people to remember you were a shining light or negative when you leave the room?

Who has your back? Look in the mirror.

Who are you giving a piece of your heart to?

Stop giving away your gifts. They are valuable and have a price tag beyond money-think about it.

Your thoughts of yourself will help you succeed- or not.

You can be beautiful on the outside and open your mouth and turn ugly - be mindful.

Keep moving forward to win.

To be truly beautiful or handsome, your heart must be focused on blessing.

You are powerful enough to make a difference.

Learn a skill such as selling and never go hungry.

Understanding we all learn differently, instead of getting loud and frustrated, rephrase your words and re-explain.

Look back on the people who impacted your life and write them a note of thanks.

True happiness is _____.

Money is nice, but time is priceless.

Passion will take you farther than dreaming.

What's your next move?

Your past hurts that you bring into new situations can prevent you from seeing the good.

What words make you melt? Repeat them to yourself.

You do not need someone in your life who is focused on negativity.

When you stop taking daily action, you extend the time it takes to achieve your goals.

Goals

What do you want to do with your life?

YOUR DAILY BOOST

If something catastrophic were to occur in your life, what is the one thing you would mourn that you had not achieved?

Look for signs from the universe. Sometimes, you need a tap or push to open your eyes.

Be cautious of your daily routine. Repeating the wrong actions will become a habit.

Remember, you are in control of your response.

When you say yes to many activities and can no longer focus on your goals, it's time to make you a priority.

Are you getting your proper rest daily?
For real?

Are you all in and excited until it's time to put in the work?

Success

When fear of success shows up, ask yourself, is this a fact or assumption?

Never throw someone else under the bus to elevate yourself.

People go through life worrying about others' opinions, and this is the wrong way to go about it.

Master your process, and you will find success.

Following up strategically will result in new beginnings.

YO, you are equipped with everything you need to be successful. We may need to make a few tweaks, but you got this. Ready set go!

Today is GO MODE. Let's go one step at a time.

It's a guaranteed NO unless you ask.

It's 99% going to happen if you follow through.

You are enough. Scratch that. You are more than enough.

Are you tired of wishing for a different life? This is your sign. Today is the day to take one step at a time and make a change.

Are you showing up for Likes or to share value? It's two different things.

Planning to be successful and taking action on your plan go hand and hand.

Your age, weight, height, and current bank account have **ZERO** to do with how successful you will become.

The Biggest Gift you can give yourself is to allow yourself to be the student and then take action.

There is always someone worse off. Your situation is just a detour, not the destination.

Choose your self-talk wisely.

If you have decided you can't, you are closing the door on your dreams.

Dream Big

Remember to KISS daily, that is - Keep it Super Simple.

Determining what someone is interested in vs. focusing on your preference can be a game changer.

Remember to have a simple strategy or recipe that you follow daily. You will work less and have better results than consuming tons of free content and not taking action.

The more action you take, the more people you bless - mic drop

Stop sitting on info and not taking action. This will not change your life or business.

Hey, are you so afraid of success that you are sabotaging yourself?

Do you ever really fail if you try???

I CHALLENGE YOU to say one positive phrase daily for 30 days. Start with I Am _____ and state what you would LOVE to be your reality.

You don't lack confidence; you lack the recipe to follow.

What you speak becomes ingrained in you and ultimately becomes your reality.

Systems are predictable, and isn't that what we all crave??

Get a mentor and set up your systems. YOU can do it, BUT it starts with taking action.

Believe in yourself instead of depending on others for your happiness.

A reminder: if you want to see the fruits, you must take action.

DON'T FORGET

The day you wake up and say, "I have had enough" I am meant for more, no more wasting time.
Is the day you will be open to creating systems in your life and business that rely on strategy, NOT on emotion.

Have a mind and heart that is open to learning; it will take you much farther than being closed off. Give it a try.

Quick question: are you giving off the same energy that you want to attract?

GOOD ENERGY

YO Guess what? YOU are in charge of your success.

Hang out with those who INSPIRE YOU, LIFT YOU, and LISTEN TO YOU.

AVOID the negative peeps who bring you down. They are NOT worthy of your space.

Love yourself so much that you are not seeking approval from others.

Confidence is attractive.

Your upbringing does not determine your success in life -your actions do.

Are you pouring into your own cup or waiting for others to fill you up?

Fill your mind with knowledge and share it.

Get to a place in life where you can look in the mirror and be grateful for the changes, experiences, and wisdom vs. picking out what you perceive are flaws.

You may not be happy where you are, but remember, someone, is praying to be in your shoes.

Have a mindset of abundance, knowing there is enough wisdom, love, and success to go around for everyone.

Are you taking care of yourself or waiting for others to take care of you?

Learn random things and share them with others.

Remember that even if you're not happy with where you are now, there are people who wish they were in your position.

YOUR DAILY BOOST

Look at yourself in the mirror and be thankful for the changes, experiences, and things you have learned instead of only focusing on what you think is wrong.

Grateful!

Be happy with the experiences you have had in your life and appreciate the lessons you've learned.

Instead of wanting what you don't have, be thankful for what you do have.

Believe in yourself instead of depending on others for your happiness.

Take care of yourself and grow as a person.

Invest in yourself, and you will see the benefits not only for you but also for others.

Remember to take care of yourself first before helping others; just like they tell you on the airplane, put on your mask first.

Enjoy the journey after all the curve balls and ups and downs have made you who you are.

Do you celebrate the action you take, even if it seems small? Or do you dwell on the times things didn't go as planned?

Choose your focus. It truly makes a difference.

Today, you have an opportunity. What will you do with it? Procrastinate or Take Action?

Honestly, how many years have gone by since you said I want to stop working?

Do you allow the clock to keep ticking on your dreams for fear that you will not be able to handle success?

Take action today to build your legacy, as you don't know what tomorrow brings.

Don't put yourself on the back burner for your family.

Respect yourself.

Challenge yourself.

What others think of you is none of your business, so keep focusing on being a positive light.

Remember that what you have might be what someone else wishes for, so be thankful.

Take responsibility for your own responses.

Be both a student and a teacher, always learning and sharing your knowledge.

You get what you give- in all aspects of life and business.

Remember that you have the power to create your own future.

Purpose

Live with purpose.

We are all on a journey.

You never know who your Angel is.

YOU can do it, BUT it starts with taking action.

Hey, Guess What? You are equipped with everything you need to be successful.

Your Next Steps After Completing 'Your Daily Boost 365'

Completing this book is not the end; it's merely the beginning of a journey into a life of boundless energy, positivity, and potential. The insights and mantras you've encountered in these pages are tools to carry with you, integrating them into your daily life. But there's so much more to explore and discover. Here's what you can do next:

1. Reflect and Journal: Begin with self-reflection. Dedicate some time each day to journal about the insights that resonated most with you. How have they affected your daily decisions? What changes, however small, have you noticed in your mindset and behavior?

2. Join the Conversation: Connect with a global community of readers who are embarking on the same journey as you. Share your experiences, insights, and revelations. Dive deep into discussions and learn from others' perspectives and stories.

YOUR NEXT STEPS AFTER

3. Tune Into Our Podcast: Expand on the ideas and mantras from the book by tuning into our podcast. Each episode dives deeper into the topics, featuring interviews with thought leaders, success stories, and practical strategies for a thriving mindset. Find it at **yourdailyboost365.com**. Along with our journal and store.

4. Challenge Yourself: Set up monthly challenges based on the insights from the book. Whether it's cultivating gratitude, building resilience, or setting and achieving micro-goals, put your newfound knowledge into active practice.

5. Engage in Continuous Learning: The world of personal growth is vast and ever-evolving. Always remain curious. Read more books, attend workshops, or take courses that align with your goals.

YOUR NEXT STEPS AFTER

6. Share the Wisdom: Spread the word. Share your favorite mantras and insights from the book with friends, family, and colleagues. The ripple effect of positivity can be more influential than you think!

7. Revisit Often: This isn't a one-time-read book. Your journey and perspective will evolve, and different mantras will resonate at different stages in your life. Revisit Your Daily Boost 365 whenever you feel the need for a refresher.

Remember, personal growth is a journey, not a destination. And as you navigate the terrain of life's challenges and triumphs, know that Texroy, Erika, and the entire Your Daily Boost 365 community are with you every step of the way.

Here's to your endless growth and success!

Take care of yourself

Texroy and Erika

Made in the USA
Columbia, SC
17 April 2025